Ways into

Materials

Written by Peter Riley

W
FRANKLIN WATTS
LONDON•SYDNEY

First published in 2001 by Franklin Watts
96 Leonard Street, London EC2A 4XD

Franklin Watts Australia
56 O'Riordan Street
Alexandria, NSW 2015

Series editor: Rachel Cooke
Assistant editor: Adrian Cole
Series design: Jason Anscomb
Design: Michael Leaman Design Partnership
Photography: Ray Moller (unless
otherwise credited)

A CIP catalogue record for this book
is available from the British Library

ISBN 0 7496 3958 X

Dewey Classification 620.1

Printed in Malaysia

Picture credits:
Ace Photo Agency/Martin Lipscombe p. 13, Alexis
Sofianopoulos p. 24l; Corbis Images pp. 25b and 25c;
Image Bank/Inner Light p. 7; Pictor International p. 24c;
The Stock Market/Lester Lefkowitz pp. 24r and 25t
Thanks to our models:
Jordan Conn, Nicola Freeman, Charley Gibbens,
Alex Jordan, Eddie Lengthorn,
Henry Moller and Rachael Moodley

Contents

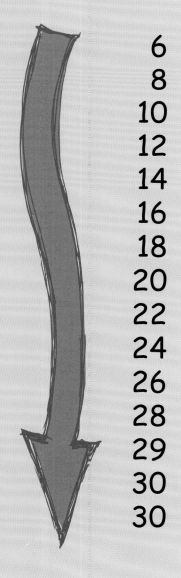

Different materials

There are many kinds of materials.

This T-shirt is made from a type of plastic called acrylic.

These trousers are made from cotton.

These shoes are made from leather.

The drainpipe is made from plastic.

The window is made from glass.

The door is made from wood.

The wall is made from brick.

Cotton, leather, plastic, brick, wood and glass are materials.

One material may be used to make very different objects.

This brush,

bottle,

toothbrush

and fork

are all made of plastic.

This key,

nail,

paper clip

and tray

are all made of metal.

We use our senses
to find out
about materials.

We use our eyes to see
the colour of materials.

This wood
is brown.

This brick
is red.

This rock
is grey.

10

We use our skin to touch and feel
the surface of a material.

This rock
has a rough
surface.

This apple
skin has
a smooth
surface.

We call the things that describe
a material its properties.

Colour, roughness and smoothness
can all be properties of a material.

What properties do your clothes have?

Hard or soft

Hardness or softness can be properties of a material.

Nadia has some materials.

metal

wool

wood

cotton

She is going to sort them into a hard group and a soft group.

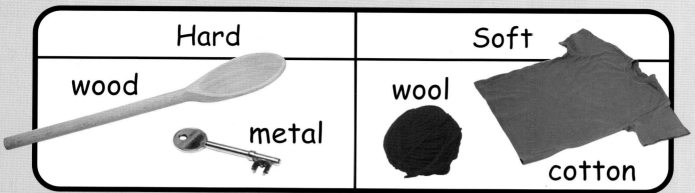

Hard	Soft
wood · metal	wool · cotton

A cotton T-shirt feels soft when you wear it.

Why has hard metal been used to make this armour?

What other materials are hard or soft?

Rough or smooth

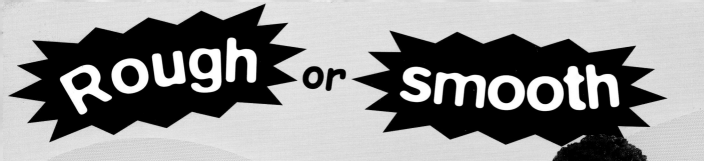

A material may be rough or smooth.

A material which is rough feels bumpy and uneven.

A scourer is rough. It cleans off dirt.

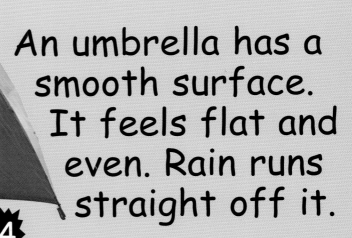

An umbrella has a smooth surface. It feels flat and even. Rain runs straight off it.

14

Toby is sorting these materials.

He is going to put them in a rough group and a smooth group.

plastic

sandpaper

cardboard

metal

glass

dough

Where will he put each one?
Turn the page to find out.

Sorting out

Rough	Smooth
cardboard	dough
	glass
sandpaper	plastic
	metal

Toby sorts the materials again.
This time he puts them into a bendy
group and a rigid group.

16

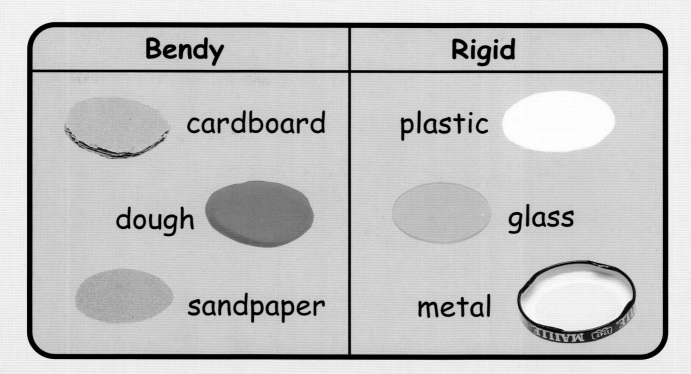

Bendy	Rigid
cardboard	plastic
dough	glass
sandpaper	metal

Plastic can be bendy like these bags.

Plastic can also be rigid like these pens.

Can metal be either bendy or rigid?

Which will stretch?

Some materials stretch.
Some materials don't stretch.
Here are two groups of materials:
one stretchy, one not.

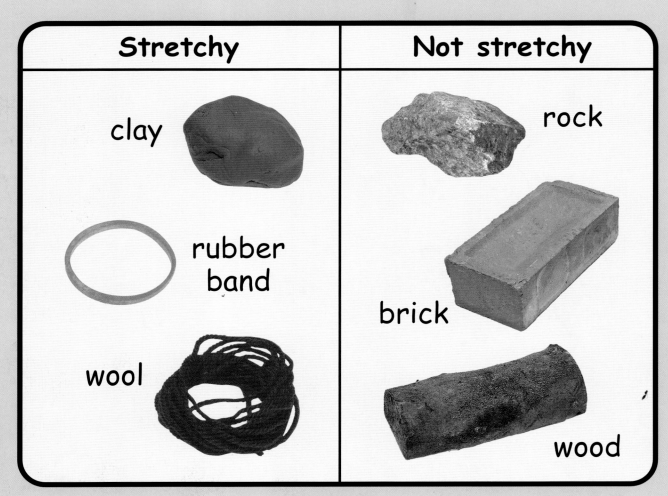

Stretchy	Not stretchy
clay	rock
rubber band	brick
wool	wood

Wool is used
to make hats.

The hat
stretches to
fit your head.

Can you think
of any other
reasons why wool
is good for
making hats?

Why is brick
not used to
make hats?

See **through** this!

You cannot see through some materials. They are opaque.

Brick, cotton and wood are opaque materials.

Most clothes are made of opaque materials!

You can see through some materials. They are transparent.

Glass is transparent.
It is used to make windows.

It lets you
see outside.

It lets light
into the
room so you
can see
inside.

What other properties of glass
make it useful for windows?
Turn the page to find out about one.

Glass windows keep the rain out.

They do not let water pass through. They are waterproof.

Find some more waterproof materials with this test.

1. Cover a table with coloured paper.

2. Lay out six materials. We used plastic, glass, cardboard, metal, cotton and paper.

3. Put a few drops of water on them.

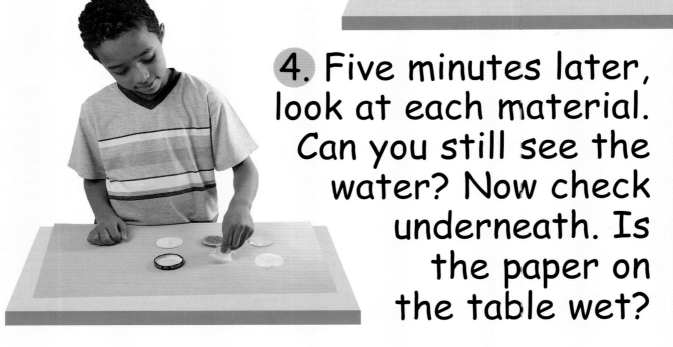

4. Five minutes later, look at each material. Can you still see the water? Now check underneath. Is the paper on the table wet?

The paper is dry under the glass, cardboard, metal and plastic. It is wet under the cotton and paper.

Which materials are waterproof?

Natural or made

Materials are natural or they are made.
Wood, wool and clay
are natural materials.

Natural materials are changed by
people into lots of useful things.

24

People mix natural materials to make new ones. These are made materials.

Paper is made from wood and other materials.

Glass is made from sand and certain types of rock.

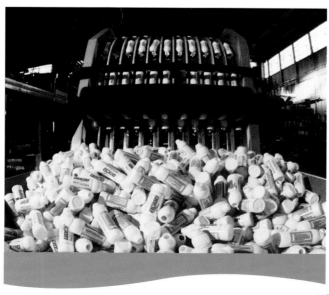

Plastic is made from oil that is found in the ground. Plastic can be moulded into lots of different shapes.

Material  hunt

Collect different objects
from around the room.

lunch box

pencil case

paint brush

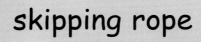

skipping rope

toy car

Look at other
objects in the room
too – for example,
a chair or a door.

Decide what material each object is made from. Make a record of your results on a table like this.

	fabric	glass	paper	plastic	metal	wood	properties
lunch box				✓			smooth and hard
skipping rope	✓					✓	bendy/rigid and smooth
paint brush				✓	✓	✓	bendy/ rigid
pencil case				✓	✓		soft and smooth
toy car				✓	✓		hard and smooth
chair	✓					✓	?
door		✓				✓	?

What properties do you think the chair and door have?
Are most objects made of more than one material?

Useful words

made material - a material produced in a factory by people. It is usually made by mixing natural materials together.

natural material - a material that is found naturally in the world around us.

opaque - not see-through. Wood is an opaque material.

properties - things that describe a material. One material has lots of different properties – for example, glass is hard, smooth and transparent. We can find out a material's properties by using our senses.

rigid - not bendy. Brick is a rigid material.

senses - we have five senses: taste, touch, smell, sight and hearing. We find out about the world around us using our senses.

transparent - see-through or clear. Glass is a transparent material.

waterproof - when a material will not let water pass through it. An umbrella is made with waterproof material.

Some  answers

Here are some answers to the questions we have asked in this book. Don't worry if you had some different answers to ours; you may be right, too. Talk through your answers with other people and see if you can explain why they are right.

page 11   This answer depends on what clothes you are wearing. What colours are they? Are they soft? Do they keep you warm? Look at their labels to see what material they are made from.

page 13   The armour is made of metal so that it protects the soldier inside from the blows he might receive in a fight. Hard materials include: rock, brick, glass and some types of plastic. Soft materials include: unbaked clay, wool, silk and tissue paper.

page 17   Like plastic, some metal can be bendy and some rigid. Aluminium foil is bendy but a steel girder is rigid. Sometimes metal, like a fork, is rigid but it will bend if you are strong enough!

page 19   Wool is also good for making hats because it is soft and helps keep you warm. Brick is not used to make hats because it is hard and heavy. It will not stretch to fit your head.

page 23   The materials which stopped the paper underneath getting wet are waterproof: glass, cardboard, metal and plastic. But in our test, the water on the cardboard seemed to disappear. It soaked into the cardboard. Do you think cardboard is always waterproof? Does the thickness of the material affect the results?

page 27   Find a chair made of fabric and wood and a door made of glass and wood to answer the first question. Lots of objects are made of more than one material. Why do you think this is?

Index

About this book

Ways into Science is designed to encourage children to begin to think about their everyday world in a scientific way, examining cause and effect through close observation, recording their results and discussing what they have seen. Here are some pointers to gain the maximum use from **Materials**.

• Working through this book will introduce the basic concepts of different materials and also some of the language structures and vocabulary associated with them (for example transparent, waterproof and comparatives such as rough and smooth). This will prepare the child for more formal work later in the school curriculum.

• On pages 15 and 21 children are invited to make predictions. Ensure you discuss the reason for any answer they give in some depth before turning over the page. It is important they give a reason, even if their answer is the wrong one. Create other scenarios and get the children to predict the results again.

• Ensure that the children understand the difference between the object and the material from which it is made. Make a collection of materials, for example a log or rock on page 10, that have not been shaped into objects.

• Develop the information on senses (pages 10-11) further. For example, put a collection of objects into a draw-string bag and get the children to describe the materials just by touch, using words explored in the book, such as soft or hard.

• Use the activity and table on page 27 to explore the advantages of using more than one kind of material to make an object.